Raising Peaceful Kids

A Parenting Guide to Raising Children in a Mindful Way

by Kathy Walsh

A *Joy Oh Boy* Book

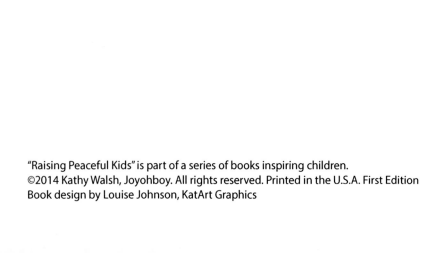

thanks

My daughters Kara Walsh and Kayle Hope
for all the lessons you taught me

Sue Bourque ~ editing and creative design

Louise Johnson ~ graphic design and production

Sarah Wheeler ~ editing

Kristin Bundesen ~ moral support

Trip Rothschild ~ love

Meredith Astles ~ marketing and partnership skills

Published by *Joy Oh Boy* Books
www.joyohboy.com

preface

"Oh what a beautiful morning, oh what a beautiful day I've got a wonderful feeling everything is going my way." I love that song. I grew up with my mom singing me that song every morning. Positive, upbeat, happy and filled with love, that was my mom.

I was one of the lucky ones....

My home was filled with love. In my home, we could do no wrong; we were all perfect just as we were, and we were loved. All the kids in the neighborhood loved our house, but not because it was big...we seven siblings shared one bathroom. It was because there was love, love so thick you could feel it in the air.

I was one of the lucky ones....

It took a lifetime of searching for me to figure out that, in the end, love is all that really matters, and I am so grateful that I did. In this book, my wish is to inspire others to raise their children in an environment of love. To be conscious of teaching children that love is all there is, forgiveness allows you to move forward, gratitude is the key to a joyful life, positive thinking is a choice, what you put out there comes back to you, and most importantly, to listen to your hearts.

My dream is that children learn to meditate; they learn that they can quiet the mind, focus on the positive, ask a question, feel even the hardest feelings and let them go. I did not start this journey until I was in my 20s, and I sometimes wonder what my life would be like if I had learned these tools as a young child.

We as parents learn how to feed and take care of our children, but there's no manual on how to raise our children with an intention.

I was one of the lucky ones... *"I've got a wonderful feeling everything's going my way..."*

chapter 1

Positive Thinking

I do believe in fairytales, but this does not mean that I believe that life should be perfect all the time. In fact, it's how we handle the imperfections that counts. There are struggles, many of them. Take Cinderella for example; she begins the story in a very tough position. When things were not going very well for her, somehow she believed in the impossible. Even surrounded by soot, she kept her eye on the prize. She believed that it could all turn around, and it did. The universe will always provide the circumstances to turn challenging situations around if you just ask and believe. Positive thinking is a choice. So how do we raise children to be positive thinking beings? One way is by simply setting the example and being positive ourselves.

When I went through my divorce, my children were 11 and 13 years old. I realized that this challenging time provided a wonderful opportunity to show them that by being positive, things that seem horrible could turn out to be wonderful. I taught them never to listen to people who tell you that things are impossible. Impossible things happen every day.

My divorce was sad and I did not pretend it wasn't; I cried a lot and felt the feelings. However, I still maintained that things happen for a reason. A year after my then-husband left, I met the man of my dreams, my soul mate. He provided my girls with a wonderful life. He supported all of their hopes and dreams and allowed them to grow up to be wonderful young adults. He was the father that they never had. Now as young adults, my ex-husband, their father, has stepped up to the plate and become a part of their lives, too.

My daughters watched me turn a negative situation into a positive one simply by believing that it was possible. When children are going through a hard time, ask them to imagine the most wonderful outcome and then know that the universe will make it even better than that. They should acknowledge the feelings that arise. *"I am feeling so angry, sad, rejected at not making the first string of the basketball team, or not getting that part in the play that I wanted."* Let them feel those feelings, and then move on to imagining a good outcome. Then, watch what happens.

We can practice positive feelings with our children every day. In my book, Life Is a Rainbow, one of the activities I discuss is imagining what our rainbow looks like. Spend a moment in the morning to teach your children to set the tone of positive energy for the day. Ask them to imagine what color their rainbow is today; what does it feel like? It only takes a few minutes to help them set their day up to be wonderful. *"My rainbow is pink today! Really happy!"* Then send them off to a pink day filled with joy.

My mother used to say, *"Kathy, one day we will look back on this and laugh."* This simple sentence has given me perspective during some tough times in my life. Perspective is key to leading a positive life. Fast forward a couple of months or years into the future and look back at a situation to see something positive. Will this situation matter as much in the future? Is there a resolution?

My daughter Kara is a dancer. At the age of 13, her dance conservatory shut down and it was all an overwhelming and scary mess. We tried another dance school only to quickly realize that they did not see the potential in Kara. She wasn't happy there. One thing I really do not believe in is staying in something that is clearly not working for your child. Trust your child's inner voice. If they know it's not right, find something else. There are many opportunities out there, and the universe will provide the right thing if you just believe.

Remember Cinderella? They just showed up at her doorstep with the shoe; she did not even have to go looking for her prince.

So we found another dance studio owned by Arlene Begelman. Arlene turned out to be the best teacher we could have ever wanted. Arlene gave Kara everything she needed to go out into the professional world with confidence and to become the dancer that she is today.

A few years ago, Kara and I helped Arlene throw a party for a 30th year reunion for her dance school. We hung the decorations and photos of her students that she helped along the way. Over 150 people showed up to the event. Guess who performed? Kara. Kara always says that Arlene was one of the best things that happened to her.

So you see, sometimes it helps to believe that something better is out there and to put some perspective on your current situation. At that party, Kara and I looked back on that truly scary experience and we laughed and celebrated and danced.

Living a fairytale life means taking the tough things that life throws at you and making them positive. *"Poppycock,"* I say to the negative.

As a parent, it is not only important to be positive yourself, but also to see your child in a positive way. See them as being all that they can be, even through the times when they may be acting out. What we focus on grows; ladies this works on husbands also. Shed light on the positive aspects of your child. Even be positive about the little things.

We all know what it is like to work for someone who is always pointing out what we do wrong and reminding us of our flaws. After a while, we feel like nothing we do is right. I remember an interview Steven Spielberg did once during which he spoke about what a crazy child he was. He said that he knew his mom always believed in him. She could have told him to calm down, stop imagining such crazy things, and get down to living and conforming to the real world, but she didn't. Spielberg's mother realized he had gifts. What she really did is look at his negative aspects and see only the positive in them. Look where this hyperactive, overly imaginative kid landed.

Believe in the gifts that your child has been given. Focus on the positive. Try looking at what conventional society would call a negative as a positive. Remember, a child is never a bad child even though their actions may seem to be. I am not saying that there should not be consequences to bad behavior, but you will be surprised at what happens when you focus on the good. It grows and grows and gets bigger and better all the time. Remember the gold star you would receive when you were little? Wasn't receiving that the best feeling? How about writing your child a note and putting it in their backpack or on the bathroom mirror. *"I am proud of you for standing up for your friend on the playground,"* and add a little gold star.

Another fabulous positive thinking tool is making a collage. Take a fun colored folder and open it; get a pair of scissors, magazines, glue sticks, markers, etc. Cut out images that reflect what you and your child want to feel or see in their lives. It could be anything, from a best friend to a different house, or something as simple as a dog. Write words that describe the feelings that you and your child will feel when their lives reflect the images on the collage. Then, most importantly, hang it somewhere that you pass by and see often. I always hang the collages we make in the bathroom next to the mirror, so I see it every day…and then watch what happens.

Let's review positive thinking:

- Be positive yourself. Set the example.

- Put things in perspective. Imagine a great outcome and watch what happens.

- What we focus on grows. Shed light on the positive aspects of your child. Believe in them even when they don't believe in themselves.

- Positive thinking is a choice. Start the day off right. Take a moment with your children, close your eyes, imagine and feel a beautiful day. *"What color is your day? Today mine is periwinkle!"*

I still remember my mother singing *"Oh What a Beautiful Morning!"* at the beginning of each day.

Chapter 2

It's All About Love

I f you have ever had a dog, you know what it feels like to be loved exactly as you are. Dogs wake up every morning excited to see you. No matter what happens, they show love to you all day, every day.

Simply put, that's the deal. Parents, myself included, make a lot of mistakes, but if there is love in the home, and the child knows that they are loved exactly as they are, then all is well. This is the key. Love is the foundation by which children stand on the rest of their lives. So, how do we raise children in a loving environment? Again, by modeling behavior and by showing love ourselves. We all know what it feels like to have a best friend that loves and accepts you for who you are. It feels really good. I am lucky enough to have that person in my life. My friend, Kristin, has stood by me through the highs and the lows. I always knew that she felt the same about me, even if she did not agree with my decisions. Isn't that what we all crave so much in life? Unconditional love and acceptance.

We are all connected through our feelings and through our hearts. When you wake up in the morning, before the day gets hectic and busy, spend a moment visualizing your child. Picture them surrounded by light, and then go to your heart and send them love. This is really powerful; you will be surprised by how much this grows. You can visualize the color around them changing as you send them love. Color is something that comes to me easily, so when I visualize my children, I may start with a white light, but as I send them love the light changes to gold and sometimes pink. The bonus in all of this is when you send love out like this, it comes back to you, and then you feel love throughout your day, too. It seems really simple, doesn't it? If you are consistent and do this every day, it does work. Your child will feel loved, and isn't that what it's all about anyway?

On your way to school in the morning, stop for a moment to observe some of the beautiful things on this earth. Teach them to show love and gratitude for the trees, the sky and the birds. Often when I am hiking and I hear a bird chirping, I pause and thank it for adding music to my hike.

My daughter's babysitter Robyn is a very special human being and we are still friends with her today. She had a special compassion towards animals and now writes a blog called Raising Vegan Kids. I honor her commitment to teaching kids the value of being compassionate human beings. In our house, my dogs were a part of the family and that is the way they were treated. Our dogs came on outings with us and were loved and cared for with so much joy. Pets are a great way to model compassion, gratitude and love for other living creatures.

My daughter, Kayle, made a trip to Bhutan to help lead media literacy workshops. The goal was to give the Bhutanese students the skills they need to interpret the media that was newly allowed in their country. Bhutan is the happiest country on Earth. It is entirely Buddhist, and they actually have a measurement called Gross National Happiness. When I did some reading about the country, I was struck to discover that the Bhutanese believe that the trees, rivers and nature in general possess feelings and emotions. Due to this belief, they have created laws that require the people to treat the earth with respect. Respect is a key part to showing love because if we respect something, it shows that we value it. If you practice this a little each day, your children will learn how to respect and show gratitude and love for all living creatures, and it will reflect back to them.

One of the best compliments I've ever received came from a fellow mother. She was in the car with her then 10 year old daughter. They were driving on a beautiful fall day when her daughter said, *"Mom, look at the leaves on that tree! Isn't it the most fabulous color orange?!"* Her mom told me that she knew her daughter saw the joy in nature because she had been spending time with me. By being around me and hearing my gratitude for the earth, that child picked it up, too.

Going apple, pumpkin, or blueberry picking is one way to appreciate nature. Besides being a great opportunity for memorable snapshots, it can be a special day that your children will remember forever. We went every year from the time my daughters could walk. Walking in nature, smelling the apples, making applesauce, all of us showing love and appreciation to nature. Trust me, they never outgrow it. My daughter, Kara, who is 24, called me the other day saying it was a beautiful day in New York City and all she wanted to do was to go apple picking with me.

Love is transformational. When your child is going through a "phase" as my mother would call it, see if you can love them through it. Whether it's the "terrible twos" or the teenage years, if they feel loved, they will come out of it faster and stronger. I noticed that when my daughter, Kayle, was in high school and all of her friends would hang out at my house. When each one of them walked in, I would always look at them with so much love, seeing all the good that was inside and seeing them as all that they could be. I often would picture them at 21, having found themselves, maturing and growing into strong individuals.

Recently, one of the mothers of a now 21 year old boy came up to me at an event in town. We were talking about her son, who had grown into a fantastic young man. She said to me, "How did you know that he was going to turn out so good? We had our doubts, but you always said he was okay. Thanks for believing in him."

We recently moved from that house and the whole gang, now 21 years old, came over for the last night. All they could talk about is how grateful they were for me. They appreciated that I loved them unconditionally, and they told me how much they felt the love I gave. They got it, and that night, that love came back to me ten times over. I still have tears in my eyes when I think of it.

I have a wonderful business coach, Hal Tweedy. He has said to me over and over again, "You are going to touch many children's lives with your books." Mind you, at that point, I had not even written all of them yet, but somehow he knew. He believed in me before I believed in myself. It was his love and support that got me to where I am today. We need to somehow see our children as we know they can be. Believe in them before they believe in themselves. Since love carries an energy with it, the child will feel that love and encouragement just because you are thinking it.

My daughter, Kayle, is the best negotiator ever. She could present a case at age two that was so perfect, you just had to agree with her. Although difficult for me, I decided to encourage her gift. If she made a good, honest and strong case as to why she should get whatever, I would tell her so and let her have it.

At two years old, I used to tell her, "Boy, you would make a great lawyer." Although sometimes I wanted to tear my hair out, I could not deny that she had the skill.

I said these words with love, not sarcastically. Guess what? She recently came to me to discuss going to law school.

Let's recap:

• Love is the most powerful emotion that we have.

• See your child through the eyes of love; surround them in light filled with love.

• Teach them to show appreciation to nature and the gifts around us.

• Know that when we show love, that love comes back to us. It is the gift that keeps on giving. It's just that simple.

Chapter 3

Gratitude

Gratitude is the key to a joyful life. When you are feeling angry and having a hard time forgiving, gratitude will be there to help.

It took me five years to get pregnant. In those five years, I had a miscarriage, two abdominal surgeries, years of fertility drugs and in-vitro fertilization. It was not easy, and therefore gave me an overwhelming sense of gratitude for my daughters. I felt blessed to have them every day. When I got upset, I would remember how much I wanted them and how lucky I was to have them in my life.

"Gratitude is just a habit," I always say. Brush your teeth, make your bed and feel grateful every day. My kids kept a gratitude journal, and I loved it. When they were little, we would draw pictures of what they were grateful for. We would collect brightly colored leaves and put them in the book. This was easy and fun to do. Sometimes while driving, I would stop the car, and we would get out to look at how beautiful the sky was. I would point to the sky and say to my kids, *"Aren't we lucky to live in such beauty?"*

The bottom line is your kids learn from watching you. Acknowledging gratitude is a great way to end the day. Ask your child, *"What are we grateful for today?"* and watch the doubt, fear, anger and sadness wash away. This is a great idea for parents to do before they go to bed as well with a focus on your child. Say or write down all the things that you are grateful for in your child. *"I am grateful my child is healthy, has a great sense of humor, has a wonderful attitude towards life and is filled with energy."* Whatever they are, be grateful for that. I promise, your child will feel this positive energy, and we all know how wonderful that feels.

When my children were young, they attended the Waldorf School in New York City. I loved the nature tables they had in each classroom; I always had one in my house as well. The nature table is a designated place that to adorn with beautiful fabric, crystals, branches, flowers, rocks, pieces of a bird's nest, acorns etc. You can put a poem about nature, a bird, a Buddha, or any other special object on it. This table brings nature indoors and reminds us to be grateful for the simple beauty of what surrounds us.

I recently watched a video of a beautiful girl named Emily that was gunned down at the Newtown, Connecticut massacre. I had many feelings and deep sadness while watching this video. As I observed the father, I could see how grateful he was for the little things about his daughter. Her smile, her laughter, her eyes and her favorite color, pink. He lit up while he watched the clip of Emily, and it struck me how often as parents we take the little things for granted. When you show gratitude for the little things in your child, they will feel loved and those little things will grow because you are putting energy and thought into them. They will grow like acorns into a beautiful, solid, balanced, lovely tree.

One of my favorite quotes comes to mind:

"I am struck by the fact that the more slowly trees grow at first the sounder they are at the core, and I think the same is true for human beings. We do not wish to see children precocious, make great strides in their early years like sprouts, producing a soft and perishable timber, but better if they expand slowly at first, as if contending with difficulties and so are solidified and perfected. Such trees continue to expand with nearly equal rapidity to an extreme old age..." ~Henry David Thoreau

In my book, *Gratitude is a Funny Thing*, there is a line that reads, "Look in the mirror and see how magical life can be!" This reminds us all to see the magic that happens each day.

Chapter 4

Listen to Your Heart, Your Intuition

"Defying Gravity." I love that song from the hit musical, *Wicked.*
I listened to it over and over while I was writing this book.
It is easy to fly when you listen to your heart.

If you let your intuition guide you, your heart will soar. How do we do this with our children? Simply put, we listen to them. We teach them to respect their inner voice by giving it credibility. Listening skills are so important as a parent. After you listen to what they have to say, repeat it back to them using feeling words. If your child says that something happened to them or someone did something to them, respond using feeling words; *"You seem frustrated and hurt that this happened today."* The more we point out feelings, the more that they will begin to use those feelings and the connection to their heart will grow. If they have a decision to make, ask them how it feels in their heart if they decide one way or another. If they are unsure, have them close their eyes and take a few breaths, then tell them to visualize their heart and ask the question. See what their heart tells them. Their inner voice will probably be different than yours. By letting their heart guide them, their life will be more peaceful. Let go of your expectations and the ridiculous standards of our society. Accept your children as they are and appreciate the gifts that they bring to the world.

My husband was an extremely bright child. He was reading the *New York Times* at the age of three. He would also read the encyclopedia for fun! His father wanted him to be a physical sports guy and never appreciated what Trip brought to the world by being himself. His father was never happy with who Trip was, and therefore Trip had a hard time learning to value himself. How sad that he never learned to listen to his inner voice. He never felt good enough, and yet he had so much to give.

Trip was able to look at his childhood experience in a way that allows him to not repeat the same pattern with his own children. In fact, he did the opposite. Trip did a wonderful job accepting and loving his three girls just the way they were. He was there for them when they needed him, and he truly enjoyed every minute of it. Trip's perspective on his own relationship with his father allowed him to heal those wounds and not repeat the same pattern. Just because you did not have a loving, perfect childhood does not mean you have to repeat it.

Again, what we focus on grows.
If we value, appreciate, and hear our child's voice,
they will value and appreciate their own.

When Kayle was eight years old, she had a severe case of Lyme disease. She was not doing well, and one day she couldn't walk. We checked her into the local hospital where they transferred her by ambulance to Yale New Haven Hospital in Connecticut. They ran a battery of tests, and when the doctor finally came in, he told her that under no circumstances did she have Lyme. Mind you, Kayle is a tick attractor. She had ticks on her from the time I found one embedded in her head at three months old. We lived in "tick country" and had a golden retriever that brought dozens of ticks every day into our home. We always played in the woods and went on hikes and loved nature. Still, the doctor monitoring Kayle didn't acknowledge the fact that she had tested positive for Lyme disease several years in a row. After a couple of days in the hospital, Kayle said to me at the ripe old age of eight, *"Get me out of here. This doctor doesn't believe me and doesn't care about me."* I looked at her and I had to agree with her; she was right. I called the nurse to remove the IV from her arm, but the nurse said we could not leave. I simply asked her, *"Is this a prison? Because I'm leaving with my daughter right now."* We eventually found a Lyme specialist that did help Kayle get well. It would've been easy for me to say to her that the big deal, highly educated doctor knew more than she did, but he didn't. This was a great opportunity for me to show her how to honor her intuition and trust her inner voice. I never regretted doing that, ever. Kayle, now 23, is brilliant at making decisions that suit her. I often ask her opinion on what I should do. This skill has and will always serve her well. Encourage your children by listening to them.

My daughter, Kara, has mastered the ability to listen to her inner voice. Her path is very different than what one may consider the norm. She did not go to college and was home tutored all through high school. She was different, and I knew it. It was hard at times because of the expectations of our society, but I am always so proud of her when she says clearly what her needs are. She is living her dream, dancing in New York City and defying gravity every day.

"It's time to trust my instincts close my eyes and leap!" What another fabulous line from *"Defying Gravity."* Encourage who your children are by writing notes. How about putting a sticky note on the bathroom mirror? It could say something like, *"I am so proud of you for standing up for your friend"* or *"your writing on that homework assignment was wonderful."* Appreciate who they are.

You can also use art to listen to their hearts. Draw a picture of a heart and write a question. Then, write the solutions and all the feelings that come from the heart. It works every time.

"Listen to your heart and it will tell you everything you need to know. Your heart knows the way to the truth. Ask your heart a question and the answer will come to you."

~An excerpt from Tara's Message

Chapter 5

Letting Go

This one is so hard for me. I always had this need to fix everything for my children. I always thought that having good experiences in life would lead them to manifest more good things because they believed that they deserved it. This is true to a point, but you can't always control the way the world responds to you.

My youngest brother, Eddie, is a total inspiration for me. I have always adored him. He is a perfect example of taking a bad situation and placing it in a positive light, changing perspective. He went to college three months after my mother died suddenly in a car accident. Eddie was only at school a month when he was in a terrible car crash himself. Two passengers died, but Eddie and the driver survived. He broke his femur and had a 10 inch metal plate put into his leg. He broke seven bones in his wrist and was bruised and battered. He didn't have a mom to care for him. To make matters worse, Eddie played several sports and was a state champion pole vaulter. He would no longer do any of these activities. He spent most of the year in a wheelchair and on crutches, but Eddie was not a victim. He never felt sorry for himself. Instead, he decided to learn how to play golf and because his wrist was so stiff from being broken, it actually helped his game. I remember talking with him years later, at a time when he was so excited that he joined the Trump Golf Club in New Jersey. *"Eddie,"* I said, *"Mr. Trump will love you when he meets you."* He corrected me and said, *"No, Trump will love me when I win the tournament."* At the time of this conversation, he was not even in the tournament, and it was taking place that weekend. But someone got sick and Eddie was called up to play. Guess who won? Eddie did.

Eddie was loved by all of his older siblings because he was the last of seven children. My mother adored him; he could do no wrong. When my mom went into the hospital when Eddie was eight, they told her she would not live more than three months. She confided in me that during her surgery, she had an out of body experience. Now, this was before "out of body" was a popular term. My mom recounted the experience of leaving the operating table and seeing her body as she went toward the light. She saw an angel and asked if she could go back to her body until her baby Eddie was out of the house. She died ten years later, one month before his high school graduation. Her intention was to come back to the earth, and be in a body that wasn't healthy in order to raise her baby. I think somewhere deep inside, Eddie felt that. This love that she had for him helped him to survive a devastating car crash and turn it into something positive.

It's not what happens to you but how you deal with it that counts. Turn lemons into lemonade and teach your children the value of seeing the positive side. Their lives will reflect this positive energy over and over again.

the bright blue balloon

written by Kathy Walsh
illustrated by Veronica Swan

I have realized that stuff happens in life, but it is how we respond that counts and helps us grow emotionally. The important thing to do is to feel the feelings that come along. By putting our feelings in a bright blue balloon and letting them go, we allow the universe to solve the problem. We just need to trust that the universe will. If you feel feelings arise from a place of peace, the universe will dissolve them. My book, "The Bright Blue Balloon," mentions a way of dealing with feelings. "I took all my sadness, pains and fears, put them in a ball and pretended it was a bright blue balloon. Then I let it go." It really works. I have used this many times in my adult life in the past two years.

We are a nation of pills and addictions in large part because we are never taught how to feel our feelings. My sister, Terry teaches third and fourth graders in Vermont. She is an amazing teacher and I have so much respect for her. She had her class draw balloons and write their feelings inside of them and then let them go. There were many negative feelings written down on the balloons. It was great to see the students get theses feelings out. Beyond teaching the basics in education, my sister was also helping these students learn how to express their feelings. It can be hard to see your child be sad, and this may make you want to tell them to get over it and move on. But if you can hold the place so your child can stay with the sadness, it will pass. Like a wave, it will soon wash away. Instead of burying the feelings, they will be released.

There are a few ways you can help your children feel their feelings:

• **Make a batch of play dough.**

I always did this with my kids. We made it on the stove where it was nice and warm. Then we would knead the play dough. We would pound it, smash it, throw it and let the feelings move out of our bodies and into the play dough. It works, and you don't have to be a kid to try it.

• **Next bake some bread.**

Again, knead the dough, throw it, smash it, pound it, and work the feelings out through the finger tips. Then, enjoy the delicious results. Fresh baked bread; does anything smell better than that?

• **A walk helps.**

Take a walk in the park or the woods. Connecting with nature somehow makes it easy to see that there is a higher order to things. Marvel at nature, look at a tiny acorn and see a tree. Walking seems to unravel the brain and helps you move forward. Note how nature survives through storms and rough seasons.

• **Go into the garden and pull weeds.**

It feels so good. My mom used to say, *"God is in the garden, Kathy."* Plant some bulbs and talk about how they make it through the cold winter and bloom so beautifully in the spring. Working in the garden, planting and weeding really helps to get the feelings out and also has great productive results. It's a win-win situation!

We thrive through bad times; feel the feelings, talk about them, get them out and release the old energies that are there. Don't try to make it all okay. Teach your children how to deal with the bad things that come up. Feel it, put it in a bright blue balloon and LET IT GO!

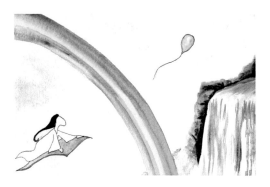

"I let go of pain and saw the light, I let go of fear and I found joy."

~The Bright Blue Balloon

Here are some tools to help encourage children to learn how to manage their emotions:

- Draw a balloon and cut it out. Write feeling words that result from a challenging situation, such as "frustrated," "angry" or "sad," on small bits of paper. Guide your child in picking out the words that best express their feelings. Let them glue the words onto the balloon. Hang it someplace visible and imagine letting the feelings go.

- With your child, close your eyes and visualize a situation that is bringing up a lot of emotion. Be sure to take several deep, slow, long breaths. Imagine placing these emotions into a balloon, and letting it go. Ask for help, wait, and trust that solutions will come.

Chapter 6

Forgiveness

This is another difficult one. I recently had lunch with a friend who, although a psychologist, said that he never really understood forgiveness. Forgiveness has many different meanings. Teaching your children to forgive, forgiving them for the things that they do, and forgiving yourself. I believe that people that truly love you (with the exception of narcissists) don't really want to hurt you. Nevertheless, their actions might be hurtful. Let's assume that children and parents both make mistakes and do things that need to be forgiven. Sometimes it seems easier to stay mad, but if you forgive your children and forgive yourself, your children will learn forgiveness. It's another win-win situation. An added bonus? Saving thousands of dollars on psychologist bills! Because instead of analyzing all the wrongs that you have done, your children will have learned and practiced forgiveness along the way.

A sad thing happened in the Mennonite community several years ago. An armed man went into the school and killed, execution style, several of the children and then took his own life. The father of one of the girls that was killed forgave the killer and actually took in the killer's family. His other daughter was having a hard time with this when he turned to her and said, *"What we hold in our hearts only grows; forgiveness allows you to live in love and let's love grow in your heart."* This is such a powerful, inspiring example of true forgiveness.

Here are some fun ways to deal with anger:

• Write a note to the person and express any and all feelings. Then crinkle it up and burn it in the sink or fireplace, or rip it up into tiny pieces and throw it away.

- Buy a piñata, hang it from a tree and hit it with a bat. Let the anger out, and then while you're forgiving, eat the candy.

If all else fails, go to Bloomingdales and shop. Only kidding!

Forgiveness does not mean that your child needs to be friends with the child that bullied them, but they do need to forgive and let it go. When things come up, seize the opportunity to teach this very valuable lesson. They need to express their anger and feel the feelings. Often, underneath the anger is another feeling that is core, like sadness. Help your child to start their sentences with "I feel." I feel sad, I feel angry, I feel hurt; whatever it is. Give them a safe place to express their feelings and get them out. Forgiveness benefits the person doing the forgiving the most. Your child does not have to forgive directly; they can forgive in their hearts and move forward without holding grudges.

If your child did something wrong, it is important that they forgive themselves, too. Parents, this is the one to practice modeling yourselves. Remember, it's a boomerang effect. Your children will forgive you too.

Chapter 7

Your Heart Knows the Way to the Truth

I dedicate this chapter to Tara.

When I was a little girl, I was panicked about separation. I was always worried about how I would survive if something happened to my mom.

I was always thinking and worrying about it, and then it happened. My mom died suddenly. I was only 24 years old, and it was six weeks before my wedding. Filled with the reality that she was gone, I began to look for ways to heal and connect. One of the ways was meditation. Meditation unlocked my mind and opened my heart. To me, meditation is the simplest way to live a more peaceful life. It is an easy way to get connected to something bigger than ourselves. I have meditated almost daily for many years.

Going to bed at night was a special time for me and my girls. Of course we would read books and talk about what we were grateful for, and then we would meditate. I loved Swami Satchidananda's meditation tape. Many nights I would lead the meditation. I would bring them to the ocean or the woods, and then I would say that we were going down steps, and then I would count down from ten to one. Within minutes, they would be in a place of peace. I highly recommend it. It doesn't take much, and it is a great habit to teach them. My kids loved it.

The past 30 years of meditating has opened up my heart and has allowed me to easily connect with my mom.

When Kara was 17, she moved into New York City by herself to dance in the Alvin Ailey professional program. This was after the September 11, 2001 terrorist attacks when there were still alerts being posted for terror activity. When Kara was living there, it seemed to me that it was almost always orange, which meant high alert. One day, she got into the subway as usual when suddenly the subway came to an abrupt halt between tracks. The ordeal lasted quite a long time. There were armed policeman walking through the trains. About 20 minutes went by and she was getting a little nervous, when she remembered the power of white light that I had taught her as a child. She closed her eyes, went into a meditation and wrapped the subway in white light. She said it was only a few minutes later when the train miraculously started moving.

I use this technique before every take-off on the runway. I wrap the airplane in light, sometimes white and sometimes a whole rainbow. For me, it creates an intention for a peaceful flight. You can do this with your children as well, especially when they are sick. Wrap them in a rainbow of light, move the light up and down their bodies, and it will clear out blockages, emotional or otherwise. Light is extremely powerful, and if you practice using it when your child is young, they will in turn use it when they get older.

Open your heart, listen to your heart, and allow your heart to guide you. Sounds easy, right? It could be, but in this society, we are raised, taught and tested over and over again on how to analyze, figure out, memorize and regurgitate information. In other words, we learn our way out of our hearts and into our heads.

"Your heart knows the way to the truth," is what Tara says in my book *"Tara's Message."* Tara, a beautiful young girl I once knew, lived in her heart. Just hours before she left her physical body, I saw her by her locker at school. *"Hi Kathy,"* she said with a big smile on her face. Although it was over ten years ago, I still have her face and voice imbedded in my memory. I then walked into the art room, turned to the teacher and said, *"Tara looks just like an angel."*

Little did I know that the next day she would become one. Tara was on a boating trip with her family. The water was rough and a tragic accident caused her to drown. I believe that our meeting that day was more than just serendipity. Tara had a message, and she chose me to send that message. It is my dream in this lifetime to let children hear this message and learn to let their hearts guide them.

When I first printed the book, I owned four retail stores. I had the books on a table in each store, and I remember watching people being drawn to the book. They would pick it up, read the words and begin to cry. The words touched their soul. Recently, I heard of a child that had passed away. Her family was given *"Tara's Message"* by the funeral director. The child's sister sleeps with the book every night. This means everything to me. To know that this child was comforted in some way by the message in this book made me feel so joyful.

Tara's message is that we are never separated, because we are all connected through our hearts. But children won't learn how to connect with their hearts in school; this is something that needs to be reinforced at home. Developing a skill takes practice. The more you listen to your heart, the better you get at it.

Here's how it works:

Take a moment, close your eyes and take three deep breaths. Now connect with your heart, breathe, imagine your heart and now take some white light and put that in the center of your heart. Ask a question and see what your heart says. What is the first thing you hear? Don't go to your head; stay in your heart and believe the answer. Then truly listen to the answer, and you will be surprised how right the answer is. Trust the answer. The more you trust it, the easier this will become.

Try it on a small decision. Maybe your child isn't sure whether to be on the soccer team or cheerleading squad. Do this with your child and let their hearts guide them. Give them the tools to trust their intuition and let it guide them.

When I became a parent, the prevailing thought was that *"you can have it all."* There was a famous New York Magazine cover of a woman in a suit holding a briefcase, diaper bag and baby, all while hailing a cab in New York City. They made it look so easy, but it wasn't, not for me anyway. It broke my heart to leave my child in someone else's care while I went to work. After all, what could be more important than raising my child, I thought. So I asked my heart what should I do, and the answer was very clear. My heart told me to be there for my girls, greeting them after school, guiding them through life, going to the beach, art classes, hikes and being active in their schools. For me, every day of being with them was heaven, and I am glad that I listened to my heart. I would never be doing the work with children that I am doing today without that life experience. Everyone has their own path in life and letting their own hearts guide them gives them their unique vision and experiences in this lifetime.

I love the quote from Steve Jobs: *"Your time is limited, so don't waste it living someone else's life. Don't be trapped by dogma -- which is living with the results of other people's thinking. Don't let the noise of others' opinions drown out your own inner voice."*

In order to hear your inner voice, we must quiet the mind. Look where listening to intuition led Steve Jobs.

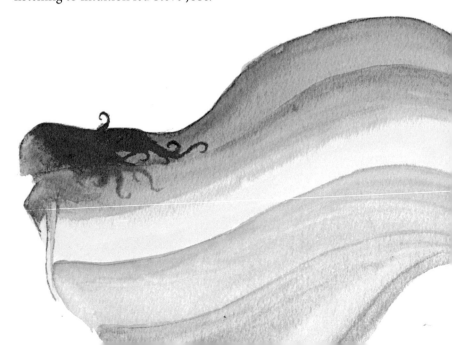

Chapter 8

The Road Not Taken

"You can be anything that you want to be," my grandmother used to tell me all the time, and I believed her! To me, it made perfect sense. I can be anything I want to be. *"Why not?"* I said to myself. In my adult life, I've been a fashion buyer, an art teacher, a graduate student recently, a PR and marketing executive for a children's school, owned my own stores, moved to Santa Fe on a gut feeling, became a social media consultant and the list goes on. Do you tell your children they can be anything they want to be? I think it's important in raising peaceful kids that they honor their inner voice. Their calling may change, and guess what? It's all okay. I would not be a children's book author today if I had not stayed home with my children all those years ago. Trust them to listen to their heart. This will lead them on their own path, no matter what it looks like on the outside.

Kayle has had an interesting path in her life. She's always had the ability to use her right and left brain at the same time; extremely creative yet technologically savvy and very methodical and smart. When Kayle graduated college, she decided with her friend Sue, an amazing, intuitive, intelligent person, to come out to Santa Fe and explore the West. They got their own apartment and started doing freelance web and graphic design. As a freelance designer, Kayle could make her own schedule and travel. She went to Burning Man, the Grand Canyon, Arches National Park, Las Vegas, San Francisco and many other places throughout the Southwest. Many people back East wondered what she was doing with her life. Where is that 9-to-5 job that every graduate was supposed to have? But I didn't worry; I supported her decision and encouraged her to follow her heart. When her teacher from St. Michael's called and asked Kayle to go back to Bhutan with her for a second time, Kayle was ready. She went for a month and had a wonderful experience working with youth and training teachers in media literacy. She was able to travel around the country of Bhutan and experience things that regular tourists weren't typically allowed to do. She made a video about her time in Bhutan, and when someone in Santa Fe saw the video, they asked her to be part of an organization called Happiness Santa Fe. This organization adopted the practice of GNH (Gross National Happiness) from Bhutan. The use of this measurement allows the Bhutanese government to make many decisions based on the happiness of its people, honoring nature, caring about the earth, meditating and balancing technology. Through this happiness project, Kayle has met incredible people. She was asked to give an hour talk in Santa Fe, and 70 people came to listen to her speak. At 23 years old, she commanded the room, and I was so proud of her. She spoke about a trip she took to a place in Bhutan where the cranes migrate. She was only able to go there because a Bhutanese boy took her. They do not normally let Westerners go there, but Kayle did. As she arrived in this mystical land, her guide told her they recently got electricity, and that the main reason it took so long was because they ran the wires underground so that the cranes would not be disturbed. Kayle also spoke about how students of all ages would meditate every day before the start of school. As I listened to this, tears came to my eyes, as this is my dream in America. Through this, Kayle met a professor from Stonybrook who suggested she apply to the graduate journalism program at CUNY in New York City. He told Kayle that she was exactly the kind of student they wanted. She's now attending that very program.

Let me recap for a minute: she graduated college, did not get a 9-to-5 job, moved out west, traveled all over, worked as a freelance graphic and web designer, worked with Youth Media Project in Santa Fe, Outer Voices in California and ended up at a well-respected Master's program in New York City. Remember, she did not work that 9-to-5 job! She listened to her own heart and that was just perfect for me. The *"Road Not Taken"* was my favorite poem as a child. Kayle took the road not taken and look where it got her. As my Nana used to tell me, you can be anything you want to be. Thanks Nana, for the encouragement. I still feel it from you today.

Chapter 9

Vibrate Love, Sing Songs, and Watch Movies

"Love is the moon, the stars and the sky."
Yes, it is.

In the end, what matters more than anything else is that we feel loved because that is what we remember. Love multiplies and the vibration moves through generations. Our love that we give our children today will live on in the next generation because it is a vibration and that doesn't go away.

Recently, I attended my nephew's wedding. It was absolutely beautiful. Everyone was so happy! Eating, dancing, smiling, and laughing! I looked around the room, and I felt it. I felt the vibration from my mother's showering of love. I realized that the most important thing she gave to us was vibrating through to this next generation, and I was so thrilled to see it. I got it, and the light went on. My mom had been gone for nearly 30 years, and yet her vibration of love was still in the room. It lives inside of us; it is the light inside.

When you get overwhelmed by life, work, children and stress, remember, it is the vibration of love that is the key. Not perfection.

When I wake up in the morning, I picture my children's hearts, and I send love every day. I know they feel it; a vibration resonates within them. They are in my heart, perfect, whole and complete. More importantly, they are loved, and love is all there is.

Love, love, love, love, love.

Love is all there is.

Say it, breathe it, feel it; it's all about love.

"You are my sunshine, my only sunshine; you make me happy when skies are gray. You never know dear, how much I love you. Please don't take my sunshine away." It's hard to believe, but my mom had seven children, and this is what she sang to us in the morning. *"Happy all the time."* That is how I think of my mom. Ours was the house that all the kids wanted to play in, and the reason was because my mom was positive, grateful, and happy every day. The songs we sing to our children become the fabric of their lives. Recently, I found myself singing on my walk in Santa Fe. The sun was shining and the flowers were blooming, and I found myself singing this song that my mom sang to me 40 years before. I called my brother, Michael, who lives in New Jersey, and I told him the story. Do you know what he said to me? *"I sing it every day, too."*

Michael is most like my mom in personality. He is a beautiful, happy, positive man. Perhaps I knew when I called him that he would relate to what I was saying, but I had no idea that he also sings this song to himself. I wonder if my mom knew that when she sang a simple song to us, so many years later it would still be part of our lives.

Put some thought into the songs you sing, the books you read, and the movies you watch with your children. You are planting a seed that will grow and blossom inside of them and live inside your memories forever.

"Secret Garden." My daughters and I watched that movie over and over again; I just loved it. I did not realize at the time, but I can see now that the movie highlighted values that I wanted to instill in my girls. As it turns out, the movie emphasized all of the messages in my children's books, too. It talks about the garden being alive, even though in the winter it appears dead. It speaks of the healing power of nature. Mary connects with her mother and Aunt who have left the earth and summons their help. It is with love in her heart that Mary is able to connect deeply with Collin. She uses her intuition, and in the end is able to heal Collin. You would be amazed at how watching a movie with a positive message becomes a part of the family dynamic. This movie reinforced gratitude, forgiveness, listening to your heart, and connecting with nature, all messages that are part of my children's book series.

Chapter 10

Intention + Gratitude + Love = The Recipe for Happy Peaceful Children

Intention is a force that sets everything else in motion. Intention is a powerful tool. Think about it; have you ever expressed out loud what your intention is for raising your children? I know what mine was. Very clearly, my intention was that my children would listen to their hearts and let their own intuition guide them. I wanted them to be what they wanted to be, and I have moved mountains to make that happen for them.

My daughter, Kayle, was an extremely independent child. She was way ahead of the game, and although challenging at times, I always wanted to embrace that quality in her. No one could believe the things I let her do. From jumping off the dock at the lake at two years old with the "big kids" to taking the train to New York City with her friends at 16 and ultimately letting her skip sixth grade and move to seventh grade a year early.

I heard it over and over again. *"You're not going to let her do that, she's not old enough."* But she was, and I knew it. Kayle had what it took to accomplish anything that she wanted to do. I was always grateful for who she was.

When Kayle traveled to Bhutan, she went with three other students and two professors from her school, St. Michael's College. On the day of their departure, there was a huge snow storm that grounded every flight going out of the New York City airports. For a few hours, they thought the four students would take off without their professors. Kayle's professor called her from the road in Vermont and placed her in charge. She was a year younger than her peers, but her professor knew Kayle could handle it. He told her that she was the only one he trusted to navigate the group through Delhi, India, to their hotel and fly to Bhutan the next day. They could have been in Delhi for several days without supervision and they decided to put my daughter in charge! I had to smile when she told me that because I knew she could do it too.

"What's wrong with her?" I heard that so many times about my daughter, Kara, when she was a little girl. *"What's wrong with her? Doesn't she talk?"*

Kara was a painfully shy child with major separation anxiety. She held on to my leg for dear life at all the family gatherings. The only way I could get her to go to school was to walk her to the classroom doorway where the teacher was standing. But I never thought there was anything wrong with her. I only saw her as perfect, whole and complete just the way she was. I never focused on the fact that she was shy. I would visualize her in a beautiful white light, imagining all she could be.

Then, one day it happened. I remember the moment like it was yesterday. I took Kara to ballet class with her amazing teacher, Arlene Begelman. She was about 11 years old and this clearly was her life path. Arlene tuned to me and said, *"She speaks with her body on stage. She does not need to talk because she talks through her dancing."* Wow, what a powerful statement and affirmation of what I knew already.

Now Kara dances in front of thousands of people on stage. I recently went to a party for the opening night of the musical, Oklahoma, where she had a starring role. Watching her gracefully navigate through the party as people kept congratulating her on her beautiful performance was a total joy for me. *"What's wrong with her?"* I thought to myself, *"Absolutely nothing."*

Let's recap:

- Remember your intention with raising your children.
- Say your intention out loud.
- Make a board of images that support that intention. Hang it where you will see it and be reminded of it.
- Every day, write down or say out loud what you are grateful for when it comes to your child.

epilogue

Let's agree to make this "Peaceful Soup" together.

Step 1: Throw your intention for raising your kids into the pot.

Step 2: Add gratitude for everything they are.

Step 3: Forgive yourself for not being the perfect parent.

Step 4: Be positive in front of them and listen to your own heart. Teach them the same.

Last step: Sprinkle a little love on top, then let it simmer.

I see children living more peaceful, happier lives. I see children meditating every day. I see teachers and parents recognizing positive qualities in children. I see children respecting the earth, the animals, and all they come in contact with. I see children using energy and thought to be joyful. I see parents sending love to their children and enjoying every moment of parenting. I see children using gratitude as a tool to live a happier life. I see heart connections, positive reinforcement and playgrounds vibrating with love.

"This parenting guide weaves Ms. Walsh's professional and personal experiences as a teacher and parent making for an engaging read. Full of practical tips for teaching children to be aware of their world, use their imaginations and feel peaceful.

~ Kristin Bundesen, Ph.D, educator

"It's beautiful. She's returning magic to education. In a time when everything is so quantified and test driven, it's wonderful to have the balance returned. Kathy's books are helping children find the joy in their everyday life."

~ Alison, K-8 Public School Teacher

"It is a welcome change, as a parent, to have books that connect children to their heart and give them the strength and practical tools to face life's daily challenges. Today's children are always on the move, over-booked and their days are over-planned. These books give us a quiet moment in each day to reconnect to our core values."

~ Alisa, Parent of a 3rd grader and kindergartner

Kathy has over 20 years experience working with children, the arts and education. She has designed and launched programs for children at the Rudolf Steiner School in NYC, the Connecticut Conservatory of the Arts, as well as children's outreach programs with music, art and dance

"Big Shots By Cindy" @bigshotsbycindy.com

organizations. She is currently developing a mindfulness curriculum with Fayette Academy in Santa Fe and is helping launch a new private school in NYC focused on humane education. Kathy is attending the Masters Program at the prestigious St John's College in Santa Fe. She has appeared on regional and national print and broadcast media and has written a column on arts and education. Kathy has been recognized nationally with two awards for her interactive community arts events. Her eldest daughter Kara is a dancer in NYC and her younger daughter Kayle teaches media literacy internationally while pursuing her masters in digital journalism at City University New York.

Kathy lives in New York City and Santa Fe, New Mexico.